Christmas Happiness Guide

Nico PINTO

Published by Nico PINTO, 2024.

While every precaution has been taken in the preparation of this book, the publisher assumes no responsibility for errors or omissions, or for damages resulting from the use of the information contained herein.

CHRISTMAS HAPPINESS GUIDE

First edition. September 10, 2024.

Copyright © 2024 Nico PINTO.

ISBN: 979-8224624782

Written by Nico PINTO.

Table of Contents

I would like to express my gratitude and love to my beloved family. Your support and encouragement have been the driving force behind this project and I could not have achieved it without you. I hope this book will be a way for me to show my appreciation for all you have done for me and to convey my love and affection to each and every one of you. This work is dedicated to my family, always in my heart and thoughts.

Christmas Happiness Guide

Author: Nico Pinto

Don't Go Crazy ☺

Whether you're spending the holidays with your parents, your in-laws, or your crazy Aunt Mari, our guide has tips to get through any family gathering. With everything from frugal gift ideas to easy recipes for your Christmas meal, we've got all your Christmas needs covered.

And if you're spending the holidays with kids, we've got you covered too. Our guide includes ideas for entertaining children, both indoors and outdoors, so you can keep them busy and happy during the Christmas season.

Important Note About the Language Used In This Book

I want to apologize for using non-inclusive language in my book, I realize I have written everything in the masculine and have not used language that is inclusive of people of different genders.

My intention is to write for all people, regardless of gender or identity. I thank everyone who has taken the time to read my work, and I deeply apologize if anyone has felt excluded or ignored by my use of non-inclusive language. Moving forward, I will strive to use inclusive and respectful language so that all people feel welcome in my work. Again, I offer my sincerest apologies.

Nico Pinto

Introduction

Welcome to our Christmas holiday Happiness (survival) guide! The holiday season is a time to spend with friends and family. Let's face it: it can also be a time of stress, chaos, and way too much eggnog. But don't worry, we've got you covered. Our guide is here to provide you with helpful tips and tricks to survive the holidays with your sanity (and your friendships) intact.

So, sit back, grab a cup of cocoa, and let our Christmas happiness and survival guidebook help you get through the season with flying colors. Happy Holidays! ◇ ◇

Managing Christmas Stress

<u>Delegate like a boss</u>: It's easy to get overwhelmed with all the holiday planning and preparations, so don't be afraid to ask for help! Assign tasks to specific family members and trust them to accomplish them. If you're really lucky, they might even do a better job than you.

<u>Take a breather</u>: Let's face it, the holiday season can drive even the calmest person crazy. If you're feeling stressed, take a moment to breathe deeply and remember that it's just one day of the year. Then, find a quiet corner to retreat to and take a power nap. Your family can survive without you for a few minutes, we promise.

<u>Laugh</u>: When all else fails, laughter truly is the best medicine. Whether you're laughing about your own vacation mishaps or sharing a funny story with a family member, take time to let go of stress and enjoy the moment. Plus, laughter improves your mood and immune system, so you'll feel better in no time.

<u>Kids</u>: We all love spending time with kids on vacation, right? The constant noise, the never-ending energy, the sticky footprints on everything. But with a little planning, you can keep the kids entertained while keeping your own sanity. Just be sure to include some quiet activities (like reading or coloring) in between the noisy and chaotic ones (like playing tag or hide-and-seek). And if all else fails, simply give the kids some candy and they'll be quiet for at least 10 minutes.

<u>In-laws</u>: Ah, the in-laws. The ones who are always asking when you're going to get a "real" job or when you're going to start having kids. When it comes to stress management, in-laws can be the ultimate test. Just remember to smile and nod when your mother-in-law tells you how to properly stuff the turkey. After all, she has way more experience at this than you do.

<u>Remember</u>, the holiday season is about spending time with your loved ones and creating memories that will last a lifetime. Don't let stress get in your way. If you follow these simple tips, you'll be able to manage Christmas stress with ease. Have a happy and stress-free holiday! ◈

Family Members You May Encounter

The Perfectionist: We all have that one family member who believes everything needs to be perfect, especially when it comes to Christmas decorations. If you're dealing with a perfectionist, remember to take their suggestions and try to make things look exactly the way you imagined. And if they start to get too pushy, tell them you're going for a rustic, organic look this year that doesn't involve matching snowflake placemats.

The Minimalist: On the other end of the spectrum, we have the minimalist family member who believes that less is always more. If you are a minimalist, simplicity is key. Opt for natural decorations, such as pine cones and branches, and avoid anything too flashy or overwhelming.

The DIYer: There is always the DIYer in the family who loves making their own Christmas decorations. If it's one of these family members, prepare yourself for a hands-on decorating experience. Offer to pitch in and help with their latest craft project, or provide them with the space they need to let their creativity flow.

<u>The Wild Card</u>: Finally, there's always that one family member who decides to add something completely unexpected to the mix. Whether it's a giant inflatable Santa Claus in your front yard or a bright purple Christmas tree, the best way to handle the wild card is to embrace the craziness of it. After all, what's a little family Christmas madness?

<u>Remember</u>, holiday decorating should be a fun and enjoyable experience. With a little humor and some creative thinking, you can make even the craziest family member's decorating vision a reality.

Handling Children When Decorating for The Holidays

Give them their own tree: Kids love having their own special things, so why not give them their own tree to decorate? You can set up a small tree in their playroom or bedroom and let them go crazy with the decorations. Just be sure to bring plenty of vacuum bags and a roll of duct tape to clean up the glitter and tinsel.

Give them specific tasks: Kids love to feel useful, so why not give them specific tasks to complete when decorating? You can have them hang the ornaments on the bottom half of the tree or set up the nativity scene. Just be sure to give them step-by-step instructions to avoid any mishaps (like an upside-down snowman).

Make it a game: Sometimes decorating can be tedious for kids, so why not make it a game? Set a timer and see how many decorations kids can hang in 60 seconds or challenge them to a Christmas scavenger hunt to look for hidden Christmas items. The winner receives an extra candy cane or gingerbread cookie.

Let them take the lead: Children have some of the most creative and imaginative ideas, so why not let them take the lead in decorating? You may be surprised what they come up with. Just make sure you supervise them so they don't start hanging decorations on the cat or wrapping the dog in tinsel.

<u>Remember</u>, decorating is a fun family activity and a great way to bond with your kids. With a little humor and some creative thinking, you can turn decorating into a memorable experience that your kids will remember for years to come (and you'll look back on it with a smile, too!).

Fun Tips

<u>Tasty Christmas Appetizers</u>: Looking for the perfect Christmas appetizer to impress your in-laws? Look no further, you have the collection of recipes from the Artificial Intelligence - AI available on your phone or computer, just tell it what you have in the refrigerator and you are ready, the Artificial Intelligence – AI will even tell you what you need to buy and what you should do at every turn, it includes everything from a simple spinach dip to elegant crab cakes. Don't be surprised if your mother-in-law still insists on bringing her own signature dish "just in case"...

<u>Effortless perfection</u>: If you don't want your family or friends to know that you are not an expert in the kitchen. Don't worry, you don't need to be a five-star chef to impress them. Here's a tip from a master chef: order from your favorite restaurant and put it on a pretty plate at home, and voilà! Everyone will think it is homemade and delicious. Think about it this way! Why sweat and stress in the kitchen if someone already does it for you? Plus, this way you can avoid burning down the house or making someone sick from your food. So go relax, grab some from your favorite restaurant, put it on a plate and make it look like homemade. You can even order some sides online to make dinner even more impressive! Enjoy it!

<u>Friendsgiving Party</u>: Are you hosting a Friendsgiving celebration this holiday season? Impress your friends with a turkey recipe that will have them gobbling for more. Just be sure to check out the expert advice from your private chef or Artificial Intelligence - AI chat on how to properly stuff and roast your turkey (or, you know, just wing it and hope for the best).

<u>Creative Cookie Decorating</u>: Tired of the same old sugar cookies with red and green sprinkles? Chat with various Artificial Intelligence - AI for some creative cookie decorating ideas that will impress both kids and adults. From snowman faces to reindeer antlers, your cookies will be the talk of the table.

<u>Creative Christmas Cocktails</u>: This is the season for festive cocktails! Get creative with your holiday drinks by using ingredients like cranberries, cinnamon, and apple cider. And if all else fails, just mix vodka with some random juice and call it "Santa's Little Helper" or "Rudolph's Revenge" – your guests will never know the difference.

<u>Alcoholic Hot Chocolate</u>: Honey, it's cold outside! Warm yourself up with a delicious, boozy hot chocolate that will make you forget the winter blues. From peppermint schnapps to Baileys Irish Cream, there are plenty of ways to enrich hot chocolate and make it even more enjoyable.

<u>Remember</u>, with these fun tips, and with the help of your favorite chef and the Artificial Intelligence - AIs chat, you can turn even the simplest recipe into a gourmet creation, sure to impress your holiday guests and outlast even the most stressful of holiday gatherings. So why not get creative and have fun in the kitchen this year? Your taste buds (and your family and friends) will thank you.

Christmas Soups

Here I share with you some soup recipes that are ideal for a Christmas dinner:

<u>Pumpkin and Apple Soup</u>: A delicious and comforting option to start Christmas dinner. Roast squash and apples in the oven, then cook in a pot with onion, chicken broth, and herbs. Blend everything and add cream for a creamy texture. Serve hot decorated with toasted pumpkin seeds.

<u>French Onion Soup</u>: A French classic that is perfect for a night out. Slice onions and cook them in butter until golden, then add chicken broth and herbs. Top with a slice of toasted French bread and grated Gruyere cheese, and broil in the oven until the cheese is golden and bubbly.

<u>Roasted Cauliflower Soup</u>: A healthy and delicious option. Roast cauliflower in the oven with garlic and spices until golden and tender, then blend with chicken broth and add coconut milk for creaminess. Serve hot sprinkled with chopped scallions and toasted sesame seeds.

<u>Lentil and Chorizo soup</u>: An option with a lot of flavor and protein. Cook lentils with onion, garlic and tomato in chicken broth, then add slices of chorizo and cook over low heat until everything is well integrated. Serve hot, with fresh spinach on top.

<u>Mushroom soup</u>: Roast mushrooms and onions in the oven, then cook in a pot with chicken broth and herbs. Add a touch of cream for a creamy texture and decorate with chopped parsley leaves and toasted bread.

<u>Walnut and ginger soup</u>: A delicious and different dessert to surprise your guests. Blend toasted walnuts and ginger in coconut milk with molasses and honey, then heat in a pot and serve hot decorated with toasted walnuts.

<u>Potato and Bacon Soup</u>: A comforting classic that everyone loves. Cook potatoes, carrots, onions, and bacon in chicken broth, then blend until smooth. Serve hot, with shredded cheese, chives, and croutons.

<u>Turkey Soup</u>: If you have turkey left over from Thanksgiving or Christmas, use the leftovers to make a comforting soup. Cook the turkey with onion and carrots in chicken broth until soft, then blend until smooth. Add a pinch of nutmeg and serve hot with toasted bread.

<u>Remember</u>, in the Artificial Intelligence-AI chat you can find more recipes and culinary tips to make your Christmas dinner a success.

Christmas Salads

Here are some fun and delicious ideas for Christmas salads:
<u>Arugula, Pear and Walnut Salad</u>: Combine fresh arugula leaves with juicy pear slices and crunchy walnuts. Add a touch of crumbled blue cheese and dress with a honey mustard vinaigrette. A perfect combination of flavors and textures!

<u>Spinach, Strawberry and Feta Salad</u>: Mix baby spinach with sweet strawberries and crumbled feta cheese. You can also add caramelized walnuts for a crunchy touch. Dress with a balsamic vinegar and olive oil vinaigrette. A fresh and colorful salad to brighten up your holiday table!

<u>Beet, Goat Cheese and Walnut Salad</u>: Grate raw beets and mix with arugula. Add chunks of goat cheese and chopped walnuts. Dress with an apple cider vinegar and walnut oil vinaigrette. A vibrant and flavorful salad!

<u>Kale, Pomegranate, and Parmesan Salad</u>: Massage kale leaves with some olive oil and lemon to soften them. Combine them with pomegranate seeds and parmesan cheese flakes. Dress with a lemon-honey vinaigrette. A cool and festive salad!

<u>Avocado, Mango and Shrimp Salad</u>: Mix chunks of ripe avocado with sweet mango and cooked shrimp. Also add lettuce leaves and chopped cilantro. Dress with a lime and cilantro vinaigrette. A tropical and flavorful salad to celebrate Christmas in a refreshing way!

<u>Waldorf Salad</u>: A delicious mix of flavors and textures. Pieces of apple, celery, walnuts and raisins combine with fresh lettuce. The yogurt and Dijon mustard vinaigrette adds a creamy and tasty touch.

<u>Endive Salad with Blue Cheese and Pear</u>: This salad offers a combination of sophisticated flavors! Fresh endive leaves are mixed with pear slices and blue cheese pieces. The honey and balsamic vinaigrette adds a sweet and acidic touch.

<u>Young sprout salad with strawberries and blueberries</u>: A fresh and colorful salad. Lettuce leaves, arugula and baby spinach are combined with sweet strawberries and fresh blueberries. The olive oil and balsamic vinegar vinaigrette enhances the natural flavors.

<u>Greek Salad</u>: A classic salad full of Mediterranean ingredients. Lettuce and cherry tomato leaves are mixed with cucumber, black olives, red onion and pieces of feta cheese. The olive oil and lemon vinaigrette gives it a refreshing touch.

<u>Beet and Orange Salad</u>: A vibrant and nutritious salad. Grated beets are mixed with juicy orange chunks. Baby spinach leaves add freshness. Olive oil and balsamic vinegar vinaigrette enhances the flavors.

<u>Remember</u>, the salads you mentioned are great options for Christmas dinner. Each of them offers a combination of fresh and delicious flavors that will perfectly complement your main dishes. You can choose one or several salads according to your preferences and those of your guests. Enjoy a healthy and flavorful Christmas dinner! ◈◈

Side Dishes

Here are some side dish options that can complement your Christmas dishes:

<u>Mashed potatoes</u>: A Christmas classic. Peel and boil the potatoes, then mash them with butter and milk. Season with salt and pepper to taste.

<u>Sweet Potato Puree</u>: Another healthy and delicious option. Boil sweet potatoes, mash with butter, nutmeg and cinnamon. Add a little honey if you prefer a sweeter taste.

<u>Wild Rice with Walnuts and Raisins</u>: Boil wild rice and mix with chopped walnuts, raisins and onion. Season with olive oil and salt to taste.

<u>Glazed carrots</u>: Cook carrots in a pan with butter and a little sugar until golden and tender. You can add spices like cinnamon or ginger for a festive touch.

<u>Rosemary roasted potatoes</u>: Slice potatoes and place on a baking sheet. Drizzle with olive oil and sprinkle with fresh rosemary and salt. Bake at 200 degrees Celsius for 30 minutes until golden and crispy.

<u>Roasted Broccoli with Garlic and Parmesan</u>: Cut broccoli into florets, drizzle with olive oil, minced garlic and sprinkle with grated Parmesan cheese. Roast in the oven at 200 degrees Celsius until tender and golden.

Pumpkin Puree: Boil and mash the pumpkin into a smooth puree. Add butter, a pinch of nutmeg and cinnamon to taste.

Grilled Asparagus: Marinate the asparagus with olive oil and chopped garlic. Grill until tender and lightly browned.

Garlic Bread: This is a delicious bread baked with garlic, butter and aromatic herbs. It is perfect to complement your salads and main dishes.

Remember, these are just a few more ideas to delight your guests at Christmas dinner! Enjoy preparing these delicacies! ◇◇☺

Main Dishes

Here's a list of fun main dish ideas for your Christmas dinner:

Reindeer Turkey Burgers: Mold turkey burgers into a reindeer shape using a stencil and add fun details like olives for eyes and a carrot for a nose.

Hot dog train: Place several hot dogs in the shape of a train on buns. Use peppers and vegetables to create fun little windows and wheels.

Christmas Tree Stuffed Turkey: Make a delicious stuffed turkey, but instead of presenting it traditionally, shape it like a Christmas tree. Decorate it with carrots, potatoes, and rosemary sprigs to simulate the branches of the tree.

Snowman Gnocchi: Shape the gnocchi into snowmen using two different sizes for the body and head. Add details with black olives for eyes and grated carrot for the nose.

Jumping Reindeer Meatloaf: Make a meatloaf and shape them into jumping reindeer using pretzels for antlers and black olives for eyes. Add wooden toothpicks to simulate the legs and have fun presenting it on a platter.

Roasted leg of lamb: A classic and tasty option. Marinate the leg of lamb with fresh herbs, garlic and olive oil, then slowly roast in the oven until juicy and tender. Serve with a mint or rosemary sauce.

<u>Steak Wellington</u>: An elegant and delicious dish. Wrap a beef fillet in a layer of pâté and sautéed mushrooms, then wrap it in puff pastry and bake to a crispy, golden crust. Serve with a red wine sauce.

<u>Maple Glazed Salmon</u>: Marinate salmon in a mixture of maple syrup, soy sauce and grated ginger. Roast in the oven until tender and glazed. Serve with a creamy maple-lemon sauce.

<u>Stuffed Turkey</u>: A Christmas classic. Stuff the turkey with a mixture of breadcrumbs, herbs, butter and dried fruit. Bake until the skin is crisp and golden. Serve with cranberry sauce.

<u>Roasted Vegetable Lasagna</u>: A tasty vegetarian option. Slice roasted eggplant, zucchini and peppers and use them to layer inside a pasta lasagna. Add cheese and a homemade tomato sauce. Bake until bubbly and golden.

<u>Remember</u>, these Christmas dish ideas can inspire your kitchen creations and surprise your guests, but don't forget the traditional dishes that everyone looks forward to. How about asking your family about their favorite dishes and preparing them together to create an even more special experience? Have fun cooking and surprising your loved ones this Christmas!

Sweets

Here are some delicious dessert options that you can include in your Christmas party:

Apple Pie: This classic apple pie is like hugging Santa Claus in every bite. The combination of sweet apples and cinnamon is irresistible. Pair it with a generous scoop of vanilla ice cream and you have the perfect sweet treat for Christmas Eve!

Holiday Brownies: These brownies are the most delicious way to keep the holiday spirit in every bite. Add white and red chocolate chips for a touch of holiday cheer! And don't forget to garnish them with chopped walnuts to add a little crunch.

Gingerbread Cookies: What would Christmas be without gingerbread cookies? They are like little edible works of art. You can let your imagination run wild and decorate them with icing and colorful sprinkles. Your party will be filled with laughter and fun as everyone enjoys these Christmas treats!

Pumpkin Cheesecake: Pumpkin cheesecake is an absolute Christmas classic. It can't be missing from your table. In addition to being delicious, you can give it a special touch by adding whipped cream and sprinkling spices like cinnamon and nutmeg. It's the perfect combination of creamy and spicy!

<u>Peanut Butter and Chocolate Ice Cream</u>: Peanut Butter and Chocolate Ice Cream is an explosion of flavor! It will be the dessert that will make everyone fall in love with Christmas. Serve it with a generous amount of caramel sauce and chocolate chips for an even more festive touch.

<u>White Chocolate and Cranberry Truffles</u>: These truffles are a perfect combination of sweet and tart flavors. Mix melted white chocolate with chopped dried cranberries and shape into balls. Then simply let them cool and voilà! You have delicious, festive truffles.

<u>Fresh fruit tartlets</u>: Prepare a tart dough base and fill it with your favorite seasonal fruits, such as strawberries, blueberries, and kiwis. You can add a touch of fruit jelly as a glaze and decorate with mint leaves for a more festive look.

<u>Cup of chocolate mousse with red berries</u>: Prepare a soft and creamy chocolate mousse and combine it with a mixture of fresh red fruits, such as raspberries and blackberries. You can serve it in individual cups to add an elegant touch to your Christmas dessert table.

<u>Piña Colada Cake</u>: If you want to add a tropical touch to your Christmas menu, try this delicious Piña Colada Cake recipe. Combine pineapple in syrup and grated coconut in a fluffy cake batter and decorate with whipped cream and a sprinkle of toasted coconut. A tasty way to transport yourself to a paradise beach!

<u>Coffee and walnut cake</u>: If you are a coffee lover, you will love this cake. Prepare a base of chocolate and walnut biscuits and fill it with a soft coffee cream. You can decorate it with more chopped walnuts on top and a little cocoa powder.

Remember, these ideas are there to inspire you. Enjoy a Christmas full of sweetness and fun! ◇◇ These are just some ideas! I hope you find something you like and that all your guests enjoy a delicious Christmas dessert. ◇◇◇

Christmas Shopping

The Battle: Get ready to enter the Christmas battle arena! Shopping at this time of year is like a survival competition where only the bravest (and well-armed with shopping lists) will manage to survive. Stay calm, take a deep breath and remember: it's just Christmas, not an expedition into the jungle!

Keep it simple: Who needs to stress over an endless shopping list? Keep it simple with the power of money. Give the gift of cash or gift cards and escape the free-for-all of the stores. They'll thank you for it, and you won't have to unleash your inner strength to fight over the latest trendy sweater. Win-win!

The Neighbor: There's always the temptation to shop for those who aren't on our original list, like the neighbor next door who always gives you Christmas cookies. But before you commit to your Christmas budget, think about what you really need to buy and whether you can afford a little extra gift. And if you can't, just say no and repeat out loud: 'Merry Christmas, neighbor.'

The office: It can be a fun place during the Christmas holidays: colorful decorations, gift exchanges, and the chance to finally meet the person sending you anonymous emails. Also... Do you have a boss who is difficult to please? Don't worry, even Santa has high expectations. Just make sure you don't leave burnt gingerbread cookies on his desk and do a little research on his hobbies to find the perfect Christmas gift. It's all about earning the boss' good graces! But don't forget that you're still at work, so make sure you don't cross the line of what's acceptable. Happy professional holidays!

Magical world: Shopping online is like entering a magical world where you can do everything without leaving your home, including buying Christmas gifts. But be careful, because sometimes the photos can be deceptive. That sweater that looked amazing online might end up looking like something knitted by a blind man with one hand. Yes, a true 'handmade' piece of art! So, keep your eyes open and don't let the bright lights and joy of online shopping blind you.

Addictions: Shopping online seems like a brilliant idea to avoid the crowds and chaos of the shops. But be careful, because you will soon find yourself compulsively clicking on every offer and forgetting what it feels like to actually leave the house. There is a real danger of becoming a virtual shopping addict, completely forgetting the existence of the outside world. Welcome to the virtual world of endless shopping, where the only queues you will see are those for your shipping packages!

Remember, add your own touch of humor and sarcasm to make your Christmas shopping successful and full of laughter. And as for Christmas budgets, don't worry too much about them. After all, who really follows the budget we set during this time of year? Christmas budgets are like stocking stuffers: They may not be exciting at first, but you always end up needing them. So relax, enjoy the season and make your Christmas shopping full of joy and not stress."

Necessary Lists

Guests: Make a detailed list of your guests and find out all of their food preferences. This will help you cut down on mistakes and make sure that everyone has something to complain about at dinner. There's no better way to celebrate Christmas than with a good culinary drama!

Fresh Ingredients: Make sure to buy fresh, seasonal ingredients for your favorite dishes. Keep in mind that prices for these ingredients skyrocket this season, so be prepared to make a small donation to Santa's bank account.

Essentials: Don't forget to buy the foods considered "must haves" on any festive table, such as the supreme Christmas bird (turkey), the sacred pig (ham), the magic red fruit sauce (cranberry sauce) and the magic potatoes of happiness (potatoes). If someone dares to ask, "What if there's no cranberry sauce?", be sure to give them a disapproving look and tell them the story of cranberry sauce's origin in Christmas tradition three times.

Bites of Delight: If you don't have time, or just don't like to cook, you can consider some ready-to-serve appetizers. It's so much easier and gives you more time to vigorously argue with your loved ones over who played the most irritating Christmas song!

<u>Vegetables</u>: Add some seasonal vegetables to balance the meal. Carrots, Brussels sprouts, and sweet potatoes can act as symbolic trophies of your attempt to make this dinner a "healthy" event amidst all the Christmas culinary chaos!

<u>Alcoholic Beverages</u>: Don't forget to include the most important part of your Christmas shopping list, the drinks! You may never know how much you will really need, so be sure to buy plenty. And to avoid any drama at Christmas dinner, be sure to ask your guests what drinks they prefer. Some may want a delicious glass of red wine, while others may want something stronger, like an eggnog margarita. Who knows, you might even end up creating a new Christmas cocktail that becomes everyone's favorite. But remember, always in moderation: you don't want dinner to end up being more emotional than it should be, unless that's part of your family's tradition!" ◇◇◇ Have fun and have a merry Christmas full of toast!

<u>Non-alcoholic drinks</u>: Don't forget to include drinks for the little ones on your shopping list. Rum eggnog is not for them! Head to the section for non-alcoholic drinks, but just as delicious, such as tropical fruit juices, natural carbonated drinks or even sparkling water. Ask the kids what their favorite drinks are and surprise them with a special Christmas drink. Who wouldn't love a glass of 'Rudolph the Reindeer Soda', with a bright red nose of cherry syrup? So please don't put the kids on the liquor carousel. Keep Christmas fun and safe for the little ones!" ◇◇◇

It's important to remember that children should not be exposed to alcoholic beverages, and this is an opportunity to make their Christmas experience safe and fun. Have a sweet Christmas!

CHRISTMAS HAPPINESS GUIDE

<u>Remember</u>, review your options and set a budget to make Christmas dinner fun and affordable. But also, don't forget to stay calm in the chaotic queue at the market. Don't get carried away by stress and long lines. Take a deep breath and think about how delicious the feast you are preparing will be. You can even use that time to make friends in line! Share your secret cookie recipe with the person next door or start a round of Christmas carols. Remember, Christmas is a time to enjoy, even when you're waiting in an endless line at the market!

Allergies & Sensitivities

Food Allergies: Hey, did you get the memo that it's legally required that you ask about food allergies before serving Christmas dinner? Aside from being an obligation, it's also good to be a responsible host and avoid sending your guests to the hospital on a festive night. Get a grip, you're the boss of the evening, so make sure you ask your guests if they have any food allergies or restrictions of any kind. And if you don't, good luck in the emergency room.

Sensitivities: People are unique and can have different sensitivities to things like foods and smells. That's why it's important to ask about food allergies and sensitivities to Christmas smells before planning a Christmas dinner. Some people may be allergic to certain spices, dried fruits or vegetables, while others may be sensitive to chemicals in scented products and cleaning products. By asking about these sensitivities, you can accommodate the needs of each of your guests and ensure that everyone enjoys a worry-free dinner. Make sure you ask the right questions to make a hassle-free and memorable Christmas dinner! ◇ ◇

<u>Remember</u>, taking food allergies and sensitivities into account is the best thing you can do to ensure that your guests have a happy and safe dinner. Ask them about dietary restrictions before serving dinner, and remember that you are the boss of the evening (and not the boss of the hospital).

Frugal Gift Ideas

Your gifts should have meaning and not break the bank.

For mom: A baking kit with a recipe book, because these days everyone bakes bread and it is delicious; a custom-made cutting board, because she is a professional in the kitchen; or a reusable coffee filter with a fun message, because she loves her coffee and the planet.

For Dad: Get your dad a personalized photo album of all your favorite family memories and times together. You can do it online for a reasonable price and it's sure to make you smile (and maybe even bring tears to his eyes).

For your sister: Get your sister a personalized bracelet or necklace with her initials or birthstone. It's a thoughtful and meaningful gift that she can wear every day.

For your brother: Give your brother a personalized kitchen apron with his name or a funny saying. The best part? He'll be less likely to spill food on his clothes making family dinners.

For your wife: Get your wife a personalized mug with a funny quote or inside joke that only the two of you will understand. It's a practical gift that she can use every day and is sure to make her smile.

For the husband: a personalized bottle opener/keychain, because he is always the life of the party; or a beard care kit, if he has a beard, because he deserves some pampering too.

<u>For your father-in-law</u>: Gift your father-in-law a home beer making kit so he can enjoy his favorite beverage from the comfort of his home. It's a practical and thoughtful gift that he will surely appreciate.

<u>For your mother-in-law</u>: Prepare a homemade care package filled with items like homemade soaps, candles, and a soft blanket. It's a thoughtful and relaxing gift that will show her how much you care.

<u>For your kids</u>: a phone finder keychain or a Bluetooth tracking device for their phone (So they can stop calling and texting you every second to ask where they left their phone), a phone ring holder, or a personalized phone case with their name or a fun picture.

<u>For your best friend</u>: Get your best friend a DIY scrapbook or memory box filled with photos, ticket stubs, and other mementos from your adventures together. It is a heartfelt gift that shows how much you value your friendship.

<u>For your boyfriend</u>: Get your boyfriend a DIY coupon book with things he loves, like his favorite dinner, movie night, and a relaxing massage. It's a fun and thoughtful way to show him you care.

<u>For your girlfriend</u>: Make your girlfriend a DIY game night kit with her favorite board games, homemade snacks, and cozy blankets. It's a fun and creative way to spend quality time together without breaking the bank.

CHRISTMAS HAPPINESS GUIDE

<u>For your coworkers</u>: If you are one of those people who always chooses a last-minute gift for your office colleague and is afraid of not finding the perfect gift, don't worry, all is not lost! A simple pack of post-its, a mug with a funny message or a simple and personal Christmas card will make your coworker feel special, and you will feel relieved. Happy gift giving!

<u>Remember</u>, the key to a frugal gift is to think outside the box and be creative. With a little effort and consideration, you can give your loved one a gift that shows how much you care. Make Christmas dinner fun, chaotic and a little extravagant! ◈◈😁

Christmas Table

Start with a fun base: Use a festive tablecloth or table runner to give the table a Christmas touch. Add some decorations like pine cones, pine branches, and candles to spice it up.

Personalized Signs: Write each guest's name on small, colorful signs and place them in their place on the table. You can make them yourself out of cardstock or buy some at the store.

Personalized Menus: Create a personalized menu for each guest with their favorite dishes. Add jokes or funny sayings to make it more entertaining.

Drinks with Fun Names: Create some Christmas cocktails or drinks and give them fun names like "The Grinch" or "Rudolf the Reindeer." Add a dash of creativity and decorate each glass with a festive straw and an orange slice.

Avoid drama at the table: To avoid fights over places at the table, place people who get along well together. You can also randomly assign places or use a hat to do a drawing. This way, everyone will have a place at the table and you will avoid unnecessary drama.

Remember, the important thing is to enjoy the food and company during Christmas.

Children's Table

Cartoon tablecloth: Use a cartoon tablecloth for the table that children can color while they wait for the food.

Fun Menu: Create a personalized menu for kids with dishes they like and fun names like "Pizza Christmas Tree" or "Carrot-Nosed Rudolph." Make the menu interactive and allow children to decorate the names and draw the dishes.

Fun Decor: Add some Christmas decorations like snowmen, reindeer, and trees to the table that kids will love.

Board Games: Place some fun, kid-safe board games on the table so kids can play while they wait for their food.

Personalized Napkins: Have each child have their own napkin with their name or fun drawing on it. This will ensure that everyone has a place at the table.

Remember, Christmas dinner is about enjoying the company of friends and family, so be sure to have fun with the kids!

Christmas Themes

Pajama Night: We invite everyone to wear comfortable and fun pajamas.

Gift exchange according to a theme: such as exchanging favorite books or handmade gifts.

Theme Decoration: Everyone can decorate their space with a specific theme, such as "magical winter" or "Santa's party."

Ugly Hat Party: Everyone dresses up in their ugliest Christmas hat and has a competition to see who has the weirdest hat.

Cooking Contest: A Christmas competition where each person brings a dish and the best prepared food is judged.

Christmas Movie Night: Watch classic Christmas movies with popcorn, chocolate, and warm blankets.

Difficult Times

Christmas is a time to share love and joy, and what better way to do that than by helping people who need it most. Donating money, food, clothing and supplies to a good cause is a great way to do your part. You can also volunteer your time at charities or homeless shelters.

And if you can't donate or volunteer, even a smile and an act of kindness toward someone in need can make a difference. Don't let the stress of the holidays get you down and take a moment to remember how lucky you are in life, and how your help can make someone else's holiday season happier and brighter. Happy Holidays and thank you for considering helping those less fortunate!

Musical Ideas

Classic Christmas songs: Nothing like a little Frank Sinatra, Mariah Carey or Bing Crosby to create a festive and traditional atmosphere at your Christmas dinner. Make sure to select songs that are familiar to all of your guests.

Jazz music: If you want to give your dinner party an elegant touch, select some jazz songs with a Christmas twist. Jazz is a great choice to create a calm and relaxing atmosphere.

Children's carols: If you have children at your Christmas dinner, select some children's carols that the children can sing and enjoy. This will create a fun, family-friendly atmosphere at the table.

Traditional music from other countries: If you want to add an international touch to your Christmas dinner, choose some traditional songs from other countries that celebrate Christmas. This can make the dinner more interesting and educational.

Custom Playlist: Create a playlist of songs that you love and think your guests will enjoy as well. Make sure the playlist has a mix of slow and fast songs to keep the energy going.

<u>Music volume</u>: Music at a Christmas dinner should be at a moderate volume to create a festive and comfortable atmosphere. If the music is too loud, it can make communication between guests difficult, interrupt conversation, and ruin the relaxed atmosphere you are aiming for. If the music is too low, there may be awkward moments of silence and it may be less appealing to guests. Therefore, it is advisable to set the music volume at a moderate level according to the guests' tastes so that they can enjoy the Christmas dinner to the fullest.

<u>Remember</u>, music is a wonderful way to create a festive and enjoyable atmosphere at your Christmas dinner.

Congratulations

You've reached the end of this epic book on how to survive and make your Christmas a happy holiday. Now we just have one question for you:

How are you feeling?

If your answer is "exhausted," "overwhelmed," or "ready for a nap," then you're in good company. The holiday season can be a whirlwind of chaos, stress, and overwhelming emotions.

With our strategies for beating holiday stress, navigating family dynamics, and avoiding last-minute shopping chaos, you'll be able to enjoy the holiday season with a sense of humor and calm.

So, let's raise a glass to a holiday season full of joy, laughter, and a little sarcastic. Whether you're exchanging gifts, singing Christmas carols, or just trying to survive your in-laws, we hope our tips have helped you embrace the spirit of the season and enjoy every moment.

And always remember: the true meaning of the holiday season has nothing to do with the gifts, the food, or the decorations. It's about spending time with loved ones, creating memories, and spreading joy and goodwill.

So, take a deep breath, put on your ugly Christmas sweater and go out and make some amazing Christmas memories. You have this!

Christmas Happiness Guide

Author: Nico Pinto

END

Don't miss out!

Visit the website below and you can sign up to receive emails whenever Nico PINTO publishes a new book. There's no charge and no obligation.

https://books2read.com/r/B-A-UMPHC-XLKZE

BOOKS 2 READ

Connecting independent readers to independent writers.

www.ingramcontent.com/pod-product-compliance
Lightning Source LLC
Chambersburg PA
CBHW020651160726
47991CB00003B/1134